Understanding My Emotions

When I'm Scared

Understanding My Emotions

When I'm Angry
When I'm Embarrassed
When I'm Happy
When I'm Lonely
When I'm Overwhelmed
When I'm Sad
When I'm Scared
When I'm Sorry
When I'm Surprised
When I'm Worried

Understanding My Emotions

When I'm Scared

ALEXANDRA DALTON

**Understanding My Emotions
When I'm Scared**

Copyright © 2016 by Village Earth Press, a division of Harding House Publishing. All rights reserved. No part of this publication may be reproduced or transmitted in any form or by any means, electronic or mechanical, including photocopying, recording, taping, or any information storage and retrieval system, without permission from the publisher.

Village Earth Press
Vestal, New York 13850
www.villageearthpress.com

First Printing
9 8 7 6 5 4 3 2 1

Series ISBN (paperback): 978-1-62524-440-6
ISBN (paperback): 978-1-62524-382-9
ebook ISBN: 978-1-62524-138-2
   Library of Congress Control Number: 2014941250

Author: Dalton, Alexandra.

Contents

To the Teacher	7
When I'm Scared	8
Find Out More	42
Feeling Words	44
Index	46
Picture Credits	47
About the Author	48

To the Teacher

More than a hundred years ago, John Dewey insisted that the true purpose of schooling was not simply to teach children a trade but to train them in deeper habits of mind. Social-emotional learning builds on Dewey's theory further, suggesting that emotional skills are crucial to both academic performance and future success in life.

The research is definitive: emotional training is good for children! A recent study, reported in the *New York Times*, found that preschoolers who had even a single year of social-emotional training continued to perform better two years after they left the program; they were less aggressive and less anxious than children who hadn't participated in the program. Another study found that K-12 students who received some form of emotional instruction scored an average of 11 percentile points higher on standardized achievement tests. A similar study found a nearly 20 percent decrease in students' violent behaviors.

The goal of this series of books, UNDERSTANDING MY EMOTIONS, is to instill in young children a foundation of emotional intelligence. Use these books to help your students learn to understand, identify, and regulate their emotions. Give them important tools that will serve them well for the rest of their lives!

When I'm Scared

Every day, I feel lots of different things inside me. These feelings are called emotions. I have all kinds of emotions. Sometimes I feel happy, sometimes I feel sad. Sometimes I feel angry. Sometimes I feel scared.

All these different emotions are going on all the time inside me. All the while I'm talking to my friends, while I'm going to school, and while I'm eating my after-school snack, I'm always feeling something inside.

I feel scared when I think something bad might happen. I get scared when something feels dangerous. I'm afraid I might get hurt.

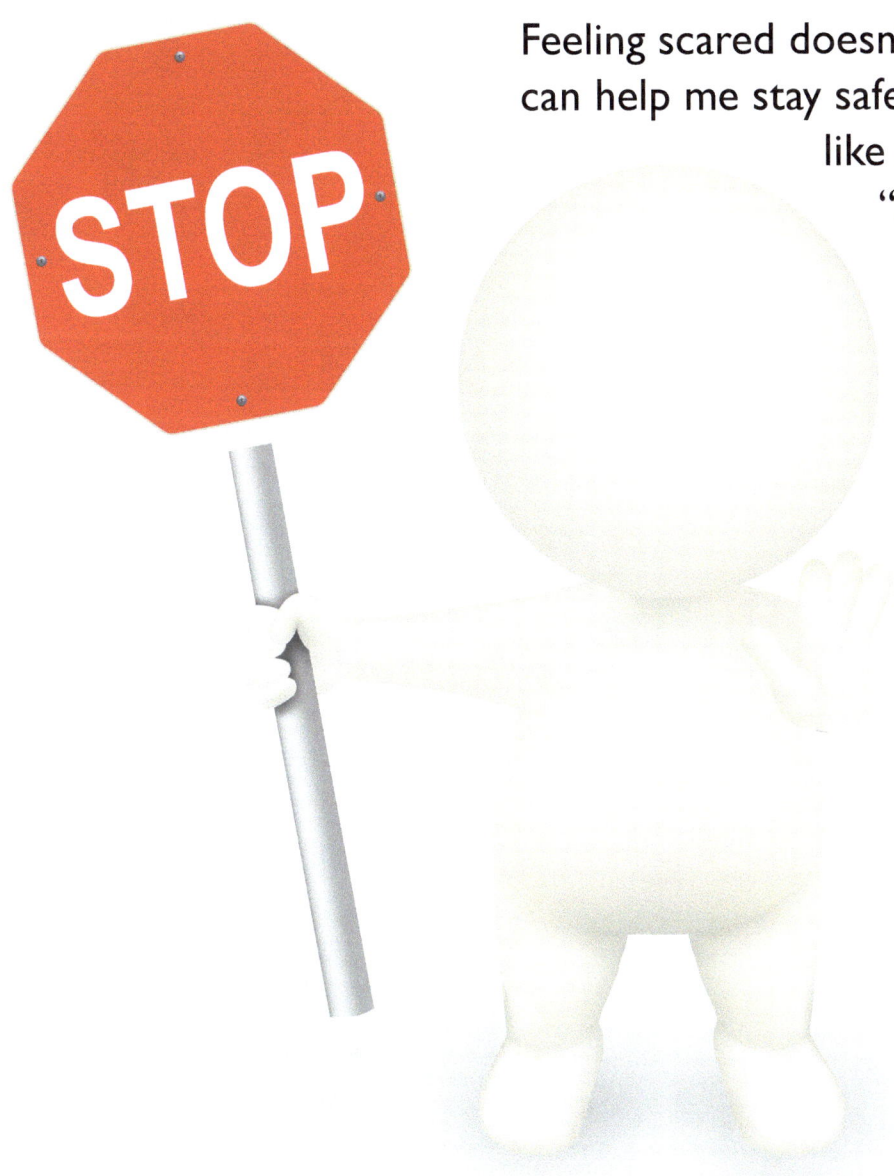

Feeling scared doesn't feel good. But fear can help me stay safe. When I feel scared, it's like a message that tells me, "Stop! Pay attention! Be careful!"

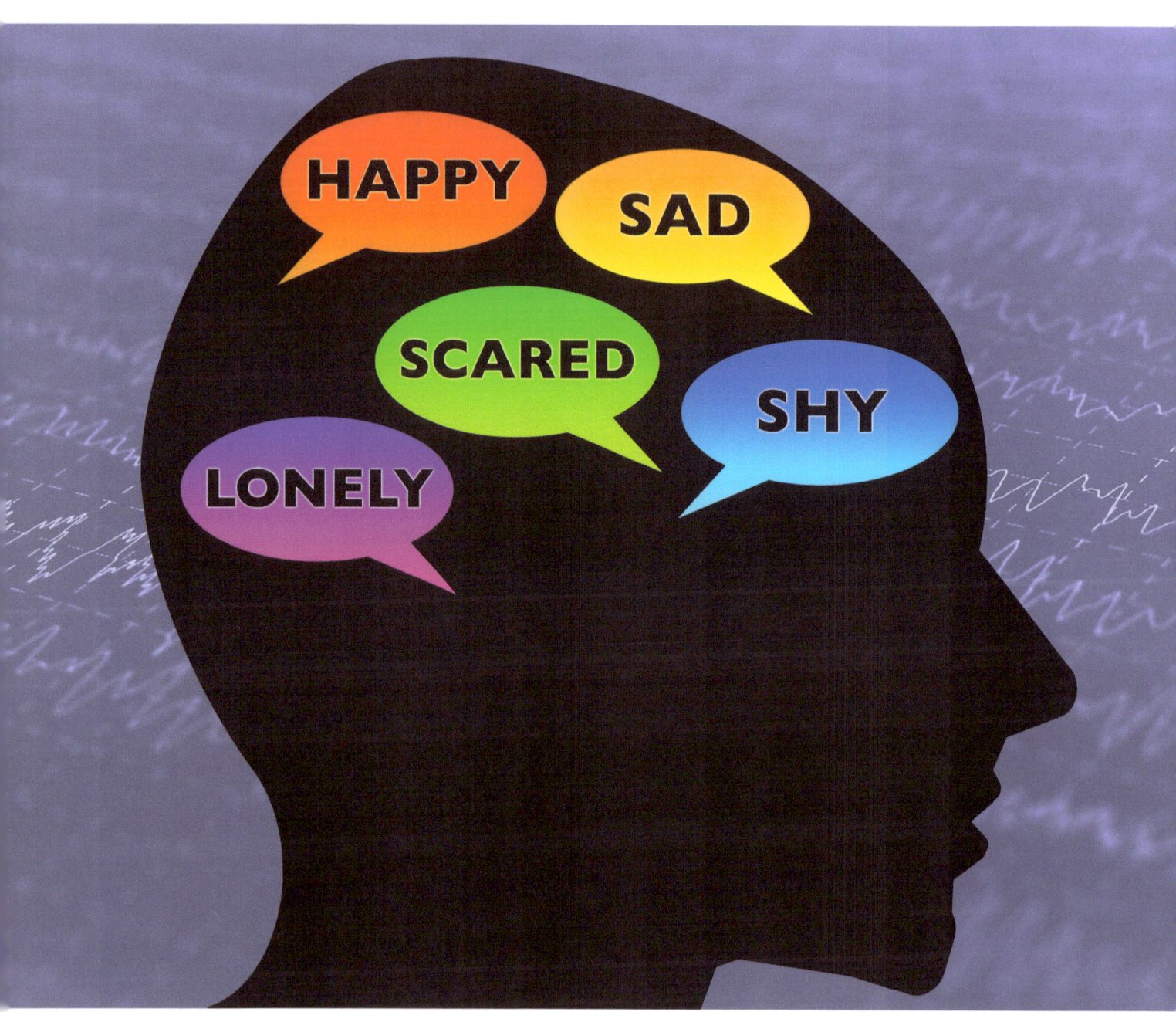

All my feelings happen inside my head.
When something happens OUTSIDE me,
my feelings happen INSIDE me. They're
like messages from inside my head that
help me know what to do next.

Inside my head is my brain. This is a picture of what my brain looks like. My brain thinks. It remembers. It comes up with ideas. It tells my body to move.

And my brain is also where my feelings happen. When I feel scared, it's because my brain has noticed that something might hurt me. Fear is how my brain lets me know I need to pay attention.

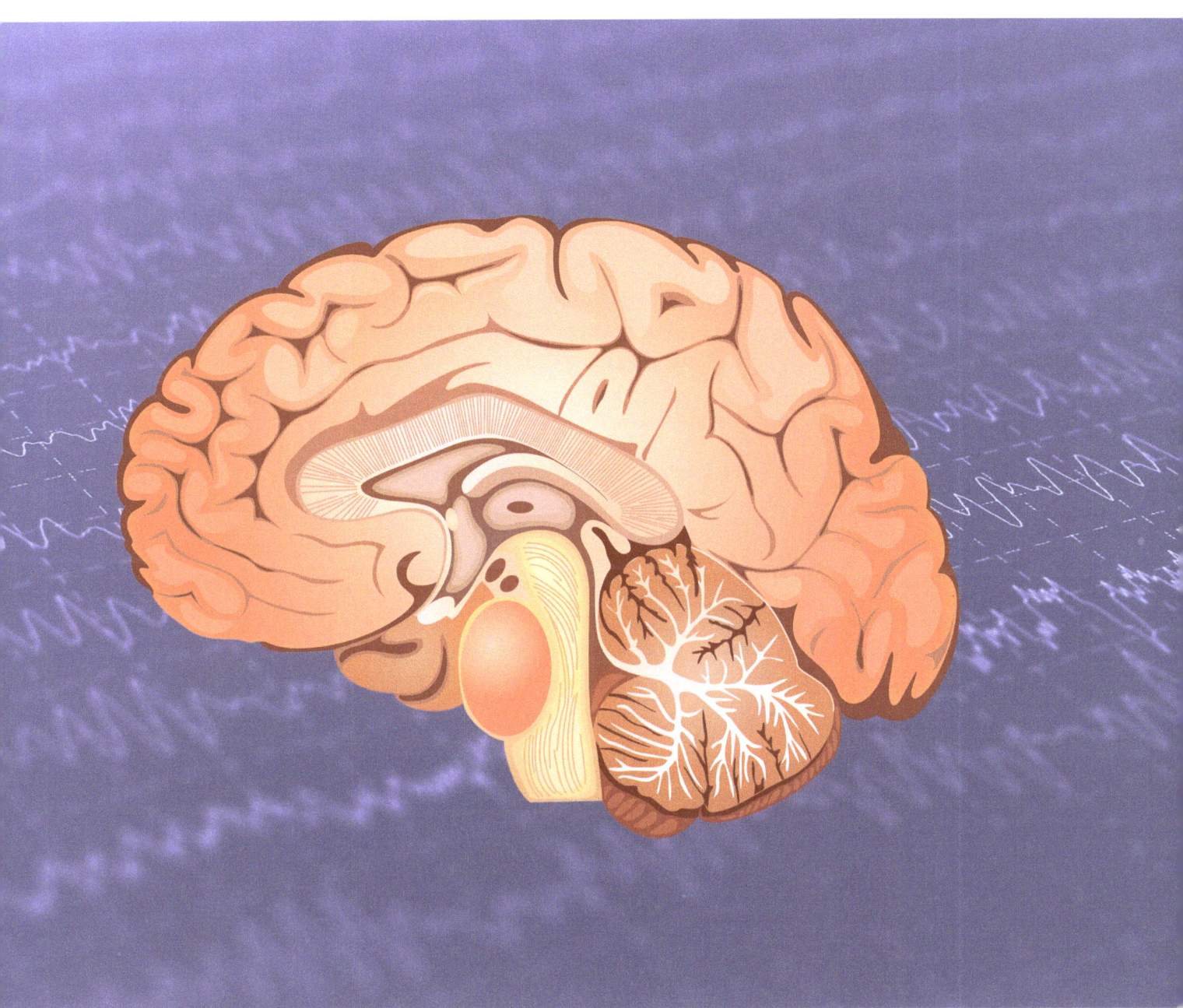

Fear is a strong emotion. Even though it starts out in my brain, it can make my whole body feel different. When I'm scared, my hands might feel sweaty. They might start to shake.

Sometimes, when I'm scared, my stomach hurts.

If I feel scared about something for too long, my head might start to hurt. Feeling scared like that means I need to get help! I need to tell a grownup what's making me so scared.

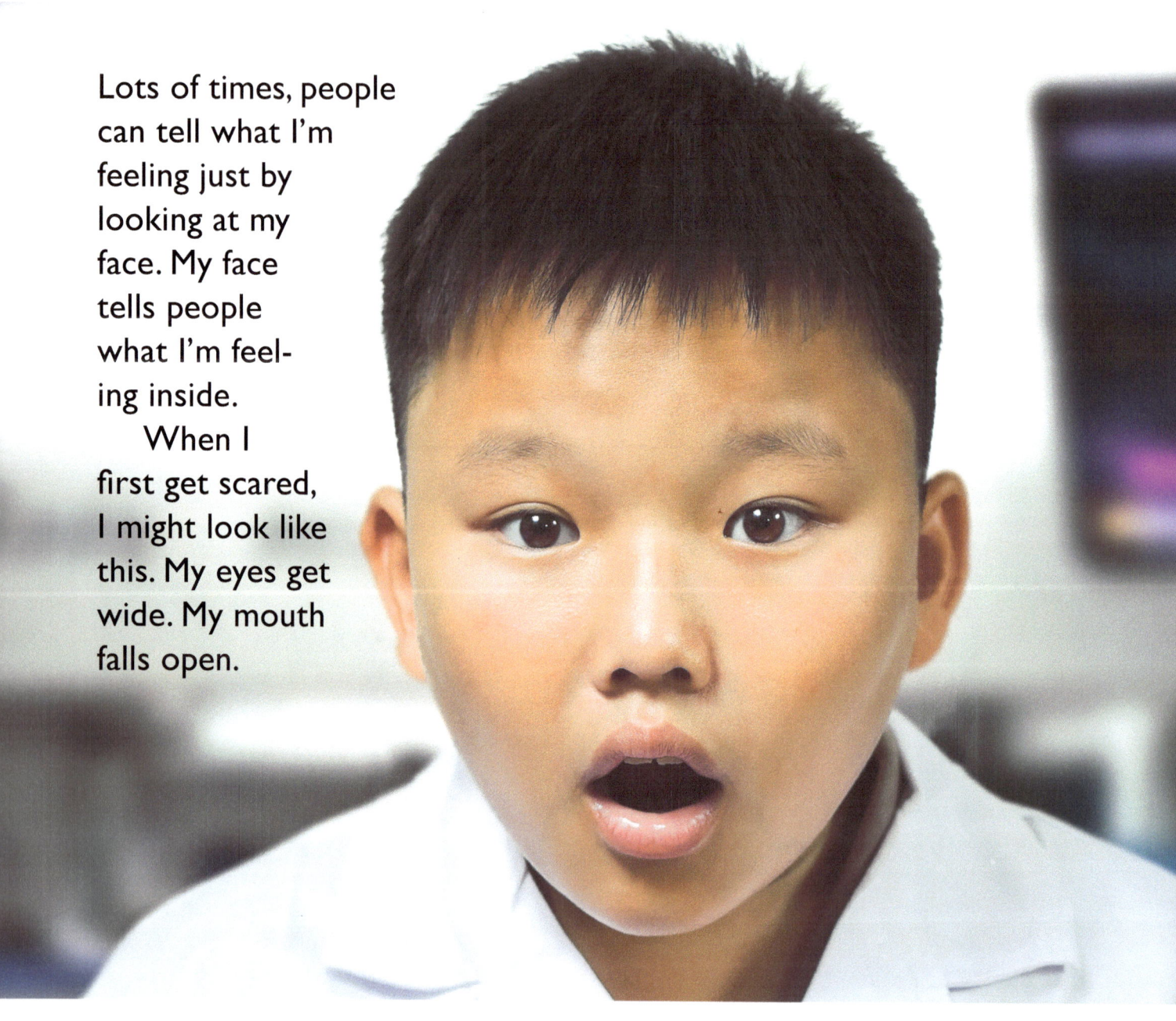

Lots of times, people can tell what I'm feeling just by looking at my face. My face tells people what I'm feeling inside.

When I first get scared, I might look like this. My eyes get wide. My mouth falls open.

I can tell what other people are feeling too by paying attention to their faces. The shape of their eyes and their mouths change, depending on what they're feeling. So when I look at my friends, their faces give me clues about what they're feeling on the inside. These clues tell me how I can help my friends.

I can tell when they're scared.

I can tell when they're sad.

I can see when they're angry about something.

And I know when they're happy and having a good time!

Grownups have the same emotions kids do. Adults feel sad and happy.

Grownups get angry when things don't go right.

And adults get scared!

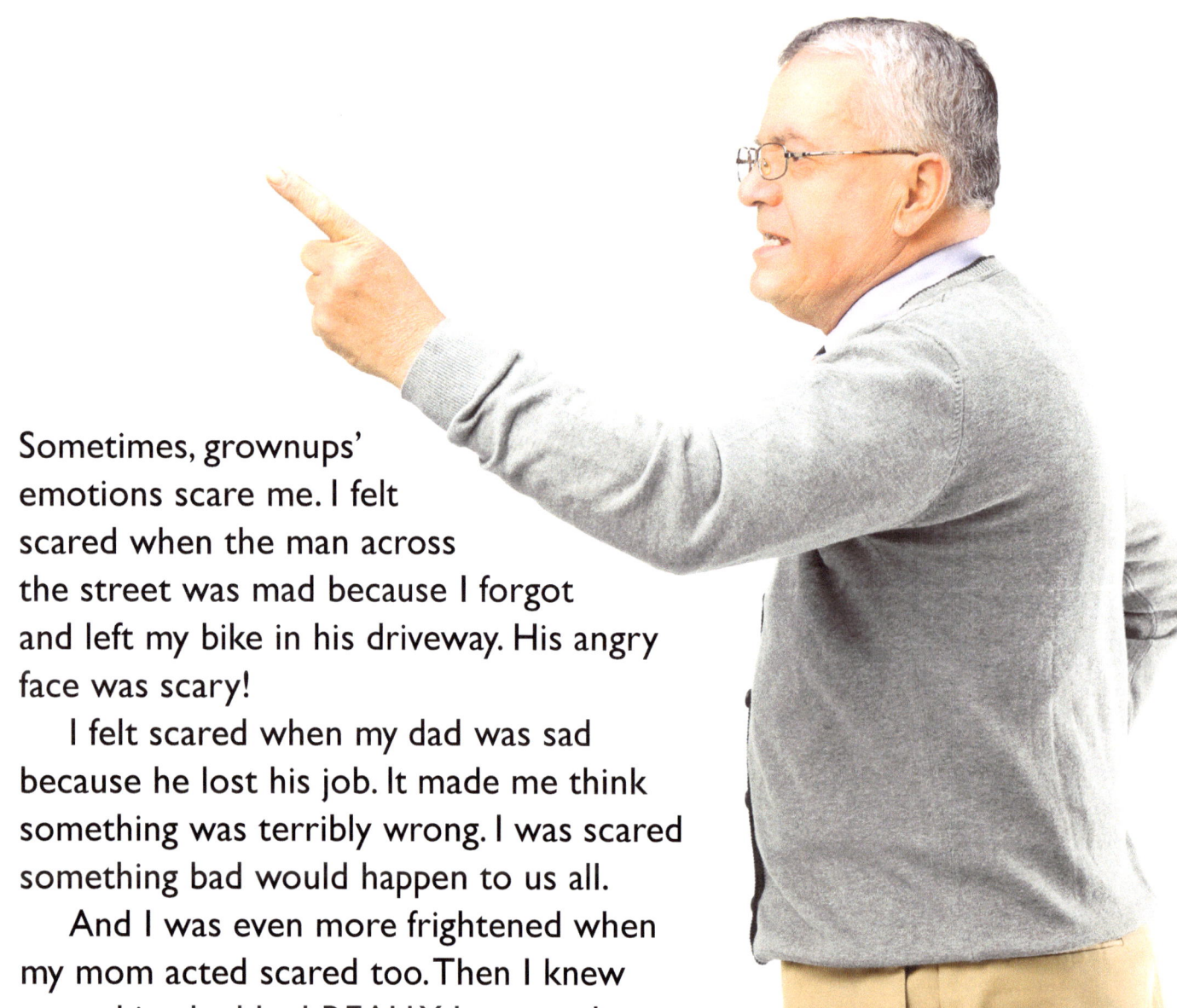

Sometimes, grownups' emotions scare me. I felt scared when the man across the street was mad because I forgot and left my bike in his driveway. His angry face was scary!

I felt scared when my dad was sad because he lost his job. It made me think something was terribly wrong. I was scared something bad would happen to us all.

And I was even more frightened when my mom acted scared too. Then I knew something bad had REALLY happened.

I just sat there and didn't say anything. I was so scared that I didn't know what to think or do.

My parents saw my face. They could tell I was upset. They told me I didn't need to be scared. They explained that grownups have feelings, just like kids do. They said that one of the big things that makes people scared—both children and grownups—is when they don't know what's going to happen next.

When my dad lost his job, my mom and dad weren't sure what would happen. They didn't know where they would get the money to pay for everything we need. That was scary for them. But they said they would work together to find an answer. My dad would look for another job. My mom would work extra hours at her job.

They told me it was a grownup problem. I didn't need to worry about it. They would always make sure I was safe. I didn't need to be scared! People can feel scared when their heads are full of questions—and they don't know the answers.

My mom suggested I call my grandma and talk to her. My grandma understood how I was feeling. She listened, and then she made me smile. Pretty soon, my scared feelings went away. My grandma said that when I'm scared, it's always a good idea to talk to someone about my feelings.

Later, my mom and I talked some more about fear. She said no one likes to feel scared—but that when we feel scared there are things we can do to get help. We talked about the different things that scare us.

I'm scared of big dogs. I'm afraid they might bite me.

My mom is scared of thunderstorms. The loud noises make her jump, and she's afraid lightning might strike our building.

Sometimes, I'm scared of taking tests at school. I'm afraid I'll get a bad grade—and that the teacher and my parents will be mad at me if I do.

My mom is scared of spiders. She doesn't know why she's scared of spiders—she just is. She thinks they look ugly. But I think they look interesting!

My mom told me it's smart to be a little scared of dogs I don't know. An unfriendly dog could hurt me, so being scared tells me to keep away from danger!

But my mom said that if I'm scared of ALL dogs, I could miss out on getting to know nice dogs. She said dogs are a little like people—I can get clues about what they're feeling from looking at their faces and their bodies. Friendly dogs hold their ears up and wag their tails.

When dogs are angry or scared, they put their ears back. They pull their lips back so their teeth show. Sometimes they growl and bark. An angry or scared dog could hurt me, so I'm smart to stay away!

My mom says the more time I spend around friendly dogs, the more I'll be able to tell when I should be careful around other dogs. She says I'll feel more comfortable with dogs. I won't be scared when I don't need to be.

I said maybe we should get a puppy like my friend Lisa's. My mom said, "We'll see!"

Then I told my mother she didn't need to be scared that lightning will strike every time she hears thunder. I explained to her that if she counts from the time she sees lightning until the moment she hears the thunder, she'll know how many miles away the lightning is. Then she'll know she doesn't have to worry. I told her there were other things she could do stay safe during a lightning storm.

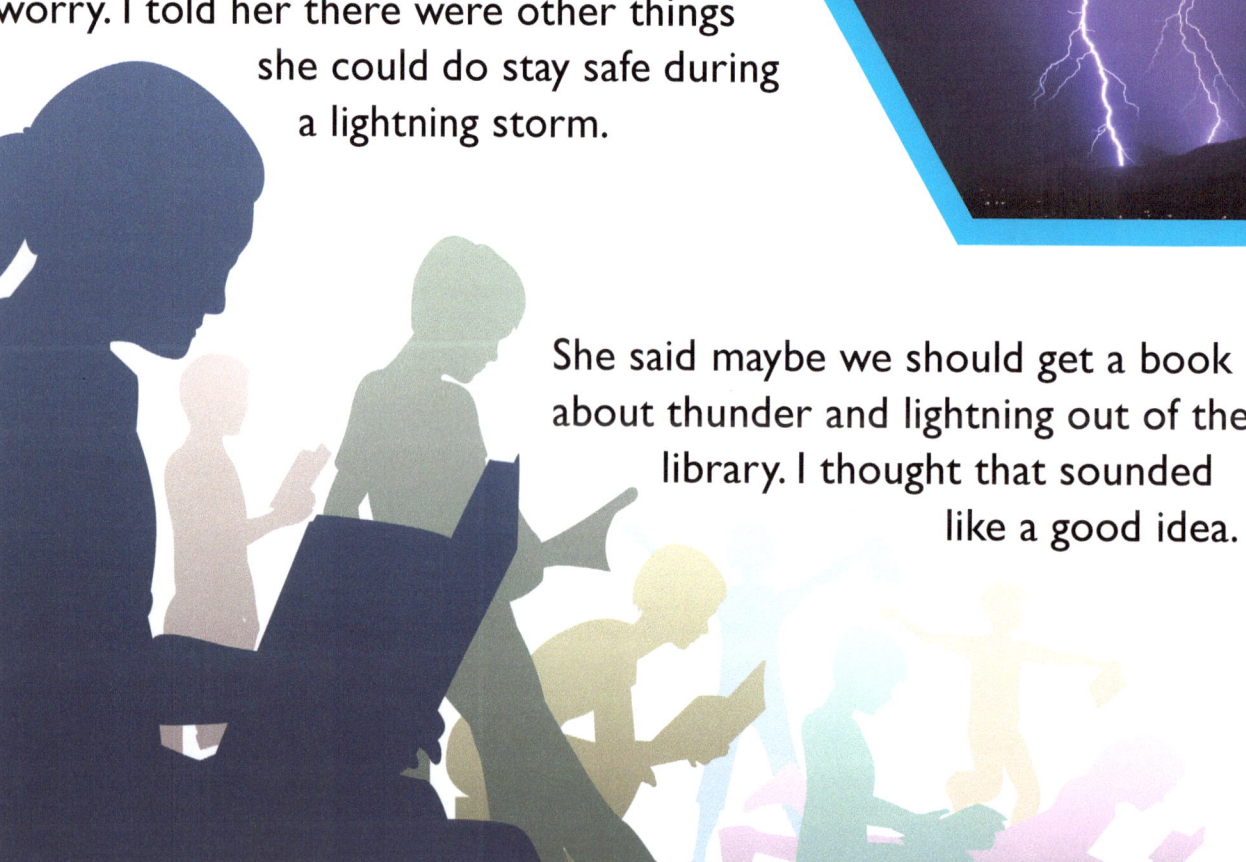

She said maybe we should get a book about thunder and lightning out of the library. I thought that sounded like a good idea.

My mom says the more we know about something, usually the less scary it seems. That's because we're scared of things we don't understand. The unknown scares us! So learning about something that seems scary at first can help our fears go away.

I told my mom she should find out more about spiders. Then she might be able to see how interesting they are. I looked up spiders on the Internet. I showed my mom pictures of spider webs. I showed her how spiders spin their webs. She agreed it was pretty interesting.

Then she asked me if I had any ideas about how I could keep myself from being scared of taking tests. I already knew the answer to that one. The more I study ahead of time, the less scared I feel during the test. I'm ready for the questions.

My mom said I should also practice taking deep breaths to help me relax. She said that when we get scared, it's hard to think as clearly. It's not as easy to remember. So if I can calm down during tests, I'll be able to do my best. My mom says when I'm taking a test, I should take my time. She said it's okay to put my head down for a minute, shut my eyes, and just breathe slowly until the scared feeling goes away.

The next day, I had to go to the doctor. I was scared. My stomach hurt. My hands felt sweaty. I was shaking.

Then I remembered some of the things I had learned about fear.

I took deep breaths to help me relax.

I reminded myself that partly what was making me scared was that I didn't understand what was happening. I didn't know what to expect. I was afraid the doctor would hurt me.

So I asked the nurse to explain what was happening. I told her I felt scared.

She was really nice. She showed me what she and the doctor were doing to make sure I was healthy. She promised they didn't need to do anything that would hurt me at this visit. She even let me play with her stethoscope! Before long, I was laughing. I didn't feel scared at all!

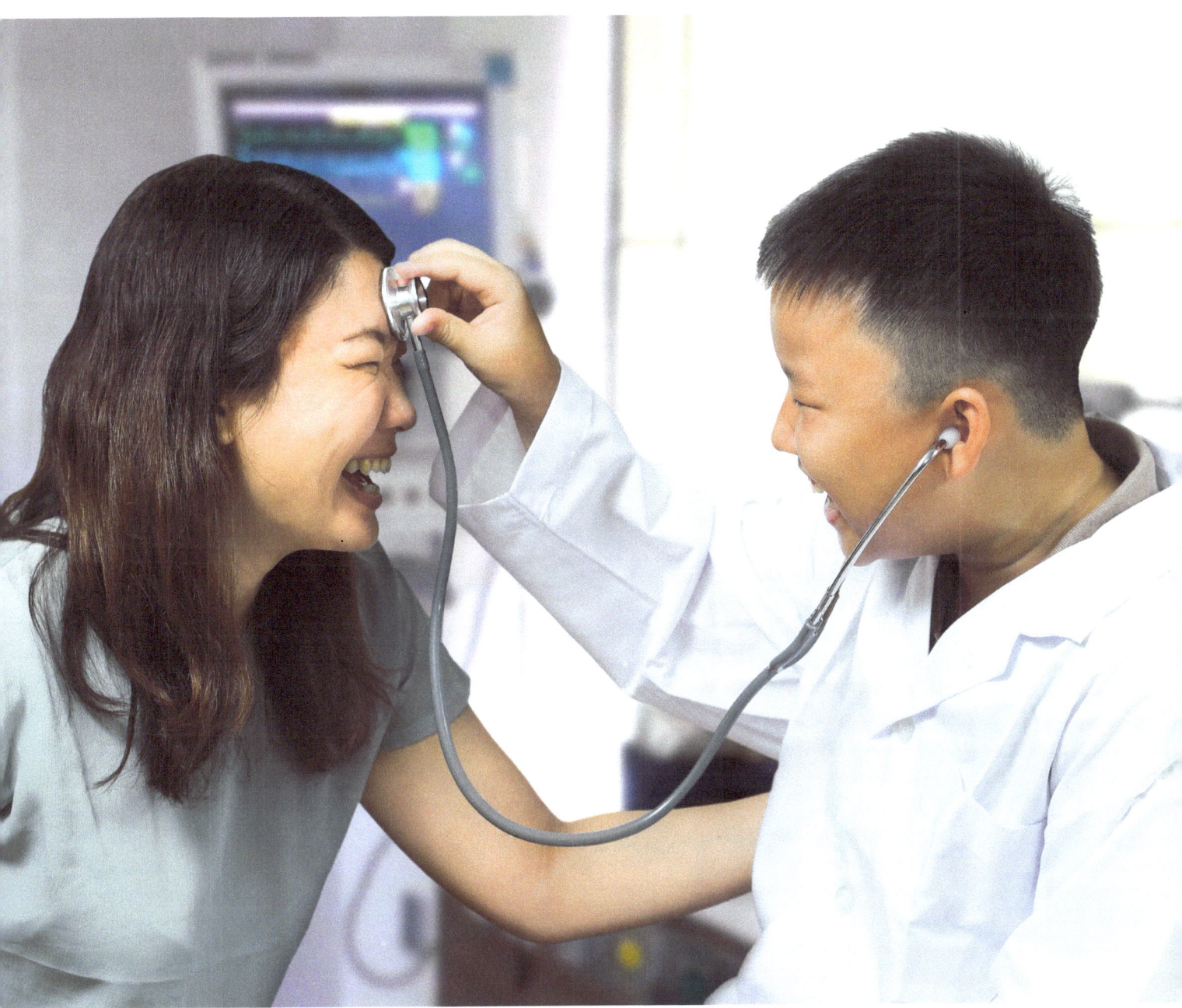

Now that I know more about fear, fear isn't as scary. Sometimes, it's even kind of fun to be scared! My friends and I like to scare ourselves on Halloween. We like to watch scary movies together. Sometimes when we have sleepovers, we tell each other ghost stories. We terrify ourselves—but it's fun!

Feeling scared is perfectly normal. It's a feeling that every person in the entire world feels sometimes.

The next time YOU'RE scared, here's what you can do:

- Pay attention. Is there danger you should stay away from? Should you be extra careful to keep yourself safe?
- Try to learn more about what scares you. Usually, the more you know and understand, the less scared you'll feel. So go to the library. Look online. Ask questions!
- Talk to someone you trust. When people know you're scared, they can help you feel better.
- Make sure you get ready for something that scares you. The more prepared you are, the less scared you'll feel.
- Take deep breaths and try to relax.
- Find something to laugh about. It's really hard to laugh and feel scared at the same time!

Find Out More

You can learn more about your emotions by going online and checking out these websites. Some of the sites have videos you can watch or games you can play. You could also read the other books in this series to find out more about feelings—or you could go to your library and see if you can find the books listed on the next page. There's a lot more you can learn about loneliness and other feelings!

On the Internet

It's My Life: Emotions
pbskids.org/itsmylife/emotions

KidsHealth: Feelings
kidshealth.org/kid/feeling

Model Me: Faces and Emotions
www.modelmekids.com/emotions_dvd.html

In Books

Crist, James J. *What to Do When You're Scared and Worried.* Minneapolis, MN: Free Spirit, 2004.

Graves, Sue. *Who Feels Scared? A Book About Being Afraid.* Minneapolis, MN: Free Spirit, 2011.

Meiners, Cheri J. *When I Feel Afraid.* Minneapolis, MN: Free Spirit, 2003.

Remkiewicz, Frank. *Gus Gets Scared.* New York: Cartwheel Books, 2011.

Seuss, Dr. *What Was I Scared Of?* New York: Random House, 2009.

Spelman, Cornelia Maude. *When I Feel Scared.* Park Ridge, IL: Albert Whitman, 2013.

Thomas, Pat. *Why Do I Feel Scared? A First Look at Being Brave.* Hauppauge, NY: Barrons, 2010.

Feeling Words

Lonely is just one of the words we use when we talk about feelings. But there are many more words that describe feelings. Here are some of those words.

Excited

Angry

Embarrassed

Worried

Guilty

Hurt

Proud

Lonely

Shy

Sorry

Surprised

Bored

Index

An index is a way you can quickly find something inside a book. The numbers tell you exactly what page to go to if you want to find that word.

angry 9, 19–20, 22, 33
attention 11, 14, 19, 41

brain 14, 16
body 14, 16, 32
book 34
breath 37

dad 22, 26
doctor 38
dog 28, 32–33

eyes 18–19, 37

face 18–19, 22, 24, 32
friend 9, 19, 33, 40

ghost stories 40
grandma 26
grownup (adult) 17, 20–22, 24, 26

Halloween 40
hand 16, 38
happy 9, 19–20
head 13–14, 17, 26, 37

laugh 41
library 34, 41
lightning 29, 34

mom 22, 26, 28–29, 31–33, 35, 37
mouth 18–19

movie 40

parents 24, 30

relax 37–38, 41

sad 9, 19–20, 22
school 9, 30
shaking 38
sleepover 40
spider 31, 35
stomach 16, 38
sweaty 16, 38

teacher 30
test 30, 36–37

Picture Credits

p. 7 © Cowardlion | Dreamstime.com
p. 8 © Corina Rosu | Dreamstime.com
p. 9 © Peter Junaidy | Dreamstime.com
p. 10 © Alain Lacroix | Dreamstime.com, Dule964 | Dreamstime.com
p. 11 © Alxhar | Dreamstime.com
p. 12 © Kasiap | Dreamstime.com, © Cowardlion | Dreamstime.com
p. 13 © Cowardlion | Dreamstime.com
p. 14 © Cowardlion | Dreamstime.com
p. 15 © Xavier Gallego Morell | Dreamstime.com, © Godfer | Dreamstime.com, © Bela Tiberiu Attl | Dreamstime.com, © Miroslav Ferkuniak | Dreamstime.com
p. 16 © Rineca Aprianto | Dreamstime.com, © Leung Cho Pan | Dreamstime.com, © Nomadsoul1 | Dreamstime.com
p. 17 © Szefei | Dreamstime.com
p. 18 © Cowardlion | Dreamstime.com
p. 19 © Cowardlion | Dreamstime.com
p. 20 © Fotosmile | Dreamstime.com, © Musguete | Dreamstime.com
p. 21 © Kostyantin Pankin | Dreamstime.com, © Plmrue | Dreamstime.com
p. 22 © Erik Lam | Dreamstime.com
p. 23 © Yuriy Zelenen'kyy | Dreamstime.com, © Wong Sze Yuen | Dreamstime.com

p. 24 © James Horn | Dreamstime.com, © Robert Adrian Hillman | Dreamstime.com
p. 25 © Cowardlion | Dreamstime.com, © Ivan Bondarenko | Dreamstime.com
p. 26 © Cowardlion | Dreamstime.com
p. 27 © Cowardlion | Dreamstime.com
p. 29 © Cowardlion | Dreamstime.com
p. 30 © Patryk Kosmider | Dreamstime.com
p. 31 © Diego Vito Cervo | Dreamstime.com
p. 32 © Erik Lam | Dreamstime.com
p. 33 © Yuriy Zelenen'kyy | Dreamstime.com, © Wong Sze Yuen | Dreamstime.com
p. 34 © Robert Adrian Hillman | Dreamstime.com, © James Horn | Dreamstime.com
p. 35 © Cowardlion | Dreamstime.com, © Ivan Bondarenko | Dreamstime.com
p. 36 © Cowardlion | Dreamstime.com
p. 37 © Cowardlion | Dreamstime.com
p. 39 © Cowardlion | Dreamstime.com
p. 40 © Patryk Kosmider | Dreamstime.com
p. 41 © Diego Vito Cervo | Dreamstime.com
p. 44 Fotolia: © Fasphotographic, © Cantor Pannato, © Andres Rodriguez, © Gabriel Blaj, © Moodboard Premium, © Halfpoint
p. 45 Fotolia: © Halfpoint, © Cantor Pannato, © Blend Images, © Zhekos, © Olly, © Wavebreak Media Micro; © Serrnovik | Dreamstime.com

About the Author

Alexandra Dalton was a teacher, and now she is a writer. When she was a teacher, she helped her students talk about their feelings. She knows that it's hard work sometimes to talk about our feelings—but she knows we feel better and we get along with each other better when we can use our words to talk about how we feel. Alexandra has three children. She also has a dog and a cat and four goats. She lives in New York State.

www.ingramcontent.com/pod-product-compliance
Lightning Source LLC
Chambersburg PA
CBHW061359090426
42743CB00002B/72